Out and About at the DENTIST

by Bitsy Kemper

illustrated by Zachary Trover

Special thanks to our advisers for their expertise:

Doug Stadler, DDS, and Lauri Calanchini, RDA
Central Sierra Regional Occupational Program

Susan Kesselring, M.A., Literacy Educator
Rosemount–Apple Valley–Eagan (Minnesota) School District

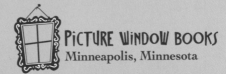

PICTURE WINDOW BOOKS
Minneapolis, Minnesota

To the Kemper family: smile, I love you!—BK

Editor: Nick Healy
Designer: Tracy Kaehler
Page Production: Lori Bye
Creative Director: Keith Griffin
Editorial Director: Carol Jones
The illustrations in this book were created digitally.

Picture Window Books
5115 Excelsior Boulevard
Suite 232
Minneapolis, MN 55416
877-845-8392
www.picturewindowbooks.com

Printed in the United States of America.

Library of Congress Cataloging-in-Publication Data
Kemper, Bitsy.
Out and about at the dentist / by Bitsy Kemper ; illustrated by Zachary Trover.
p. cm. — (Field trips)
Includes bibliographical references (p.).
ISBN-13: 978-1-4048-2278-8 (hardcover)
ISBN-10: 1-4048-2278-X (hardcover)
1. Dentistry—Juvenile literature. 2. Dentists—Juvenile literature. I. Trover, Zachary, ill.
II. Title. III. Field trips (Picture Window Books)
RK63.K46 2006
617.6—dc22
                                                      2006003442

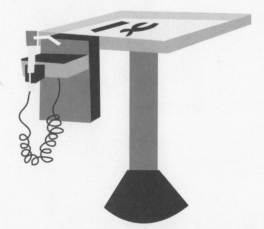

We're going on a field trip to the dentist. We can't wait!

<u>Things to find out:</u>

What happens during a dental checkup?

What is a cavity?

How do X-rays help the dentist keep teeth healthy?

What's the best way to prevent cavities?

3

Hello, my name is Geri. I'm a dental assistant. My job is to help the dentist keep your teeth healthy and clean. I'll be leading your tour of the dentist's office today.

A dentist is a doctor trained to care for teeth. At a dental checkup, we make sure your teeth and gums are in good shape.

Right now, we are at the front desk. This is every patient's first stop. That's Howard, our office manager. He keeps track of appointments and greets patients when they arrive.

A dentist is a doctor of dental surgery. That's why dentists use the initials "D.D.S." after their names.

This is our waiting room. Lots of patients come to see a dentist each day, so you have to wait your turn. We want you to relax and have fun while you are here.

We have games, books, and toys to keep
you busy. You can even watch a video.
Your wait will be over before you know it.

Dental assistants and hygienists go to special colleges for training. They spend up to four years preparing for their jobs. Dentists' education takes at least eight years.

7

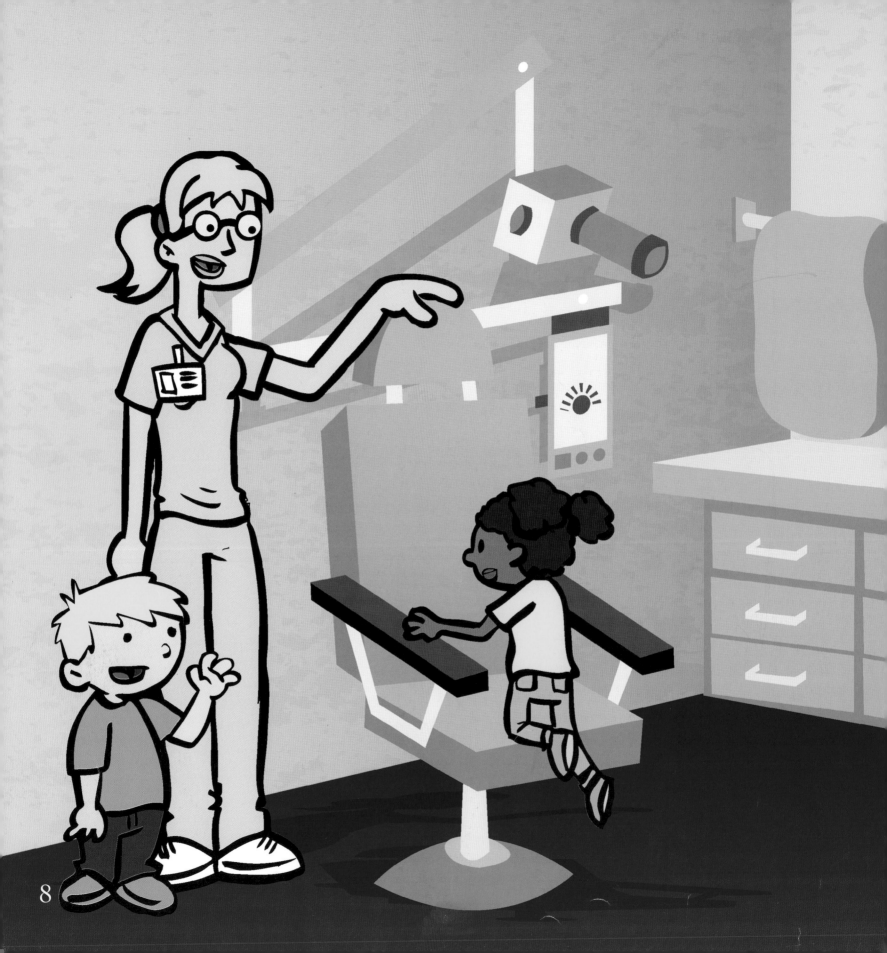

This is our X-ray room. Rachel just had X-rays taken. Our X-ray machine takes pictures of the patient's teeth and jaw. The machine works like a digital camera. We can see the pictures it takes on a computer screen right away.

We start most exams by taking pictures of your mouth. X-rays show if you have any tiny holes in your teeth. These holes are called cavities. If you have a cavity, the dentist will give you a filling.

It looks like Rachel has one cavity. We will fix that today.

X-rays show many things that are impossible to see with your eyes alone. In an X-ray, the dentist can see your whole tooth and its roots. X-rays can also show new teeth growing beneath the gums.

This is our lab. This is where we mix the material for fillings. Fillings are soft when we put them in place, but then they harden like cement. They fill holes in teeth and stop cavities from growing.

This is also where we clean all of our tools. That machine above the sink is used to sterilize dental tools. To sterilize means to kill germs. We sterilize anything that will be put in or near your mouth.

The lab is also where mouth guards get made. Rubber mouth guards can be made to perfectly fit the teeth of any person. Mouth guards protect the teeth and jaws of kids and adults who play all sorts of sports.

This is an exam room. Patients come here after X-rays are taken. Manny is a dental hygienist. Right now, Manny is cleaning Rachel's teeth and checking her gums.

Rachel is sitting in a special chair. We can raise or lower the chair, and recline it so Rachel lies flat. That helps Manny reach all of her teeth. Manny also moves the light so he can see inside Rachel's mouth.

The tray next to Manny holds some of the tools we use. The drill is in the middle. We call our drill "Mr. Whistle" because it makes a whirring sound. We control how fast the drill spins by using a foot pedal.

A paper napkin is placed over the patient's chest. It looks like a little bib. The napkin keeps the patient's clothes dry and clean while the dentist works.

This is Dr. Lucy. She is a pediatric dentist. That means she treats only children. Patients call her Dr. Lucy Toothy. Dr. Lucy checks each tooth with a little pick called an explorer. She also looks at children's teeth, gums, and jaws. Dr. Lucy fixes cavities, too.

Before she can fix the cavity, Dr. Lucy needs to make the hole a bit bigger. That way, she gets rid of the decaying part of the tooth.

For a small cavity, Dr. Lucy uses a laser to prepare for the filling. For a bigger cavity, Dr. Lucy uses the drill to clean away the decay. Then a filling goes in the hole.

The dentist's laser is silent, and the patient can't feel it. The drill can cause an ache, but dentists use a numbing medicine to help. The patient is awake, but the tooth feels like it is asleep.

This is our second exam room. Lexy's checkup is almost over. Now the assistant is brushing on fluoride. Fluoride makes your teeth strong. We ask patients not to eat or drink for 30 minutes to be sure the fluoride soaks in.

Besides fluoride, what do you think is the best way to prevent cavities? This poster has some great tips.

Take good care of your teeth today. That way, you'll have good, strong teeth when you grow up.

Avoid sugary treats.

Brush at least twice a day.

Brush after meals.

Floss daily.

See your dentist.

The average American eats about 147 pounds (66 kilograms) of sugar a year. That is more than some grown-ups weigh! No wonder the average 17-year-old has more than three decayed teeth.

This is Dr. Lucy's office. When she is not with patients, Dr. Lucy does a lot of work here. She can use her computer to see the same pictures we saw in the X-ray room. She can also look at records of patients' past visits.

18

Dr. Lucy was just looking at a new patient's X-rays. This patient may need two fillings. Dr. Lucy likes to know what she needs to do before she gets to the exam room.

Dr. Lucy keeps track of all the work she does on her patients. She wants patients to have clean teeth today and healthy teeth for life.

Foods with lots of sugar make a gooey coating on your teeth. This coating is called plaque. Plaque sticks to your teeth, and it causes cavities. Brushing can get rid of plaque.

After their appointment, patients get a new toothbrush to take home. Patients also get to pick out a sticker. Then they head back to the front desk, where they can schedule their next checkup before leaving.

20

Thanks for coming on our tour today. We've got toothbrushes and stickers for each of you. Remember to keep your teeth clean and free of plaque.

Be sure to see your dentist twice a year!

TEST YOUR TOOTH

What you need:
one (real) tooth
tweezers
one glass cup
cola
a notepad and pencil

What you do:
1. You'll need a real tooth for this activity. Maybe you saved one of yours or one from a little brother or sister.

2. Take a good look at the tooth and note the color and shape. Place the tooth in the cup. Add about 2 inches (5 centimeters) of cola—more than enough to cover the tooth.

3. Once a day, use the tweezers to remove the tooth from the cola and take a look. What is happening? Over several days and weeks, you'll see many changes. Is the color of the tooth changing? Do you see holes forming? Have they grown?

4. Keep track of the changes each day. See how long the tooth lasts.

FUN FACTS

- Dentists have been around for more than 4,500 years! An Egyptian named Hesy-Re is often called the first dentist. An inscription on his tomb in 2600 B.C. includes the title "the greatest of those who deal with teeth, and of physicians."

- A worn toothbrush will not do a good job of cleaning your teeth. Children's toothbrushes need replacing more often than adults' brushes because they can wear out sooner. You should replace your toothbrush every three or four months, or sooner if the bristles become worn.

- If you don't floss, bits of food can gather between teeth, where your toothbrush can't reach. Flossing removes plaque and food from places you can't see and brushing can't reach.

- At 3 years old, most kids have all 20 of their baby teeth. These teeth start falling out a few years later. By age 16 or so, most kids have lost all of their baby teeth and have a full set of 32 permanent teeth.

GLOSSARY

cavity—a hole in a tooth, caused by decay, or rotting

floss—a thin piece of waxy string used to clean between teeth

fluoride—a natural mineral that is applied to teeth to make them stronger and help prevent cavities

gums—the pink flesh the surrounds teeth and covers their roots

plaque—a sticky film that forms on teeth and causes cavities

X-ray—a photograph that shows bones, teeth, and other parts inside the body

TO LEARN MORE

At the Library

Adamson, Heather. *A Day in the Life of a Dentist*. Mankato,
Minn.: Capstone Press, 2003.

Keller, Laurie. *Open Wide: Tooth School Inside*. New York:
Henry Holt, 2000.

Murkoff, Heidi. *What to Expect When You Go to the Dentist*.
New York: HarperFestival, 2002.

On the Web

FactHound offers a safe, fun way to find Internet
sites related to this book. All of the sites on
FactHound have been researched by our staff.

1. Visit *www.facthound.com*
2. Type in this special
   code for age-appropriate
   sites: 140482278X
3. Click on the FETCH IT button.

Your trusty FactHound will fetch the best sites for you!

INDEX

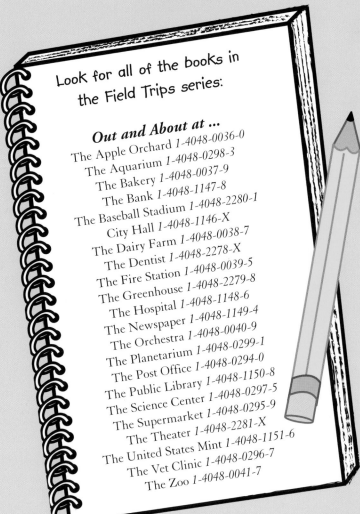

Look for all of the books in
the Field Trips series:

Out and About at ...